THIS BOOK BELONGS TO:

MaiNass

JOURNALS BY MOOREA SEAL

the 52 Lists project

52 Lists for Happiness

52 Lists
for
Happiness

WEEKLY JOURNALING
INSPIRATION *for* POSITIVITY,
BALANCE, *and* JOY

BY MOOREA SEAL

Illustrations by Julia Manchik
Photographs by Julia and Yuriy Manchik

SASQUATCH BOOKS
SEATTLE

Printed in China

Published by Sasquatch Books
20 19 18 17   9 8 7 6 5 4

Editor: Hannah Elnan
Production editor: Emma Reh
Design: Joyce Hwang
Illustrations: Julia Manchik
Photographs: Julia and Yuriy Manchik

Library of Congress Cataloging-in-Publication Data is available.

ISBN: 978-1-63217-096-5

Sasquatch Books
1904 Third Avenue, Suite 710
Seattle, WA 98101
(206) 467-4300
www.sasquatchbooks.com
custserv@sasquatchbooks.com

For my husband, Max. It is through our understanding that we can be happy on our own that we choose one another every single day. Our pursuit of personal happiness and the thought behind all that we do as individuals is the greatest foundation for loving one another well. I cannot imagine a more thoughtful and intentional yet free-spirited partner for my life than the man I love most. And it is a gift to me everyday to get to choose you over and over again.

For most of my life, I have prioritized so many things over the pursuit of my own happiness. Even the most noble and kind-hearted intentions can sometimes drive us away from the things that ground us and let us thrive. I am someone who believes deeply in investing in the people around me: friends, family, and even strangers. I set enormous goals for myself in my work and fill up my days with lists of tasks for home and the office. But it occurred to me that even when I succeed in the most difficult goals, even when I feel like I've made my community so proud, my own happiness is still not reaching its full potential. I realized that for most of my life, I have pushed happiness to the very bottom of my list of life goals. I have viewed happiness as a possible result of achieving something else, rather than allowing happiness to be the main goal.

It is so easy to forget sometimes that, just like becoming great at playing piano, just like achieving goals in work and tidying up your home, living a happy life takes intention and practice. And you know what you deserve even more than a great job, a beautiful home, or the perfect family? You deserve so much happiness and joy! It's through practicing your own individual pursuit of happiness that you achieve joy and fulfillment in all areas of your life. You are the source of your own happiness, and with weekly practice we can make that happen together! Throughout the year ahead, remember, the root of joy is already inside of you. And by taking the time to contemplate and list what makes you happy (perhaps with your favorite tea by your side and a blanket over your lap), you'll get the incredible experience of connecting to your own deepest self to create a more joyful, balanced, and positive life. Are you ready? Let's get happy!

Xo Moorea Seal

Get Together

By picking up this journal, you are already embracing and pursuing joy in your life, and the entire 52 Lists community is waiting in the wings to join you in this incredible experience! This huge group of list makers across the globe is here to support and encourage you along the way as you discover the keys to your own unique happiness. Use the hashtag **#52HappyLists** on social media to discover other people who are working their way through this journal alongside you!

If you'd like even more inspiration for self-investment, personal growth, and lots of fun through list making, check out the **#52Lists** hashtag where friends and fans are talking about what they discover and celebrate through all of their 52 Lists journals!

Would you like to see how else you can become involved in the 52 Lists community across the world? Visit **MooreaSeal.com/pages/52Lists** to learn more!

Contents

Reflect

Acknowledge

Invest

Transform

Reflect

List 1

swinging

watching inspiring videos

listening to music

laughing

hanging out with good people

making money

eating a full meal

being able to help someone

....

....

....

....

....

....

....

....

....

....

....

....

....

TAKE ACTION: How often do you actually get to experience these things? Just like learning to read, gaining the wisdom and experience of happiness just takes practice. Let's start now! Take one item on your list and see how you can turn it into a daily practice of happiness.

LIST THE ROUTINES IN YOUR PERSONAL LIFE AND WORK

....

....

....

....

....

....

....

....

....

....

....

....

....

TAKE ACTION: Circle all of the routines that bring you joy, and cross out the all the routines you dislike. What is it about the circled routines that bring you joy?

List 3

LIST THE THINGS THAT YOU ARE REALLY GOOD AT

....

....

....

....

....

....

....

....

....

....

....

....

....

TAKE ACTION: Underline the things that you had to work for to become good at, and circle the things that you feel come naturally to you. Do any of these things overlap? Just like happiness, it's already within you. It just takes practice to experience daily!

List 4

LIST THE THINGS THAT GET YOU
OUT OF YOUR HEAD

....

....

....

....

....

....

....

....

....

....

....

....

....

....

....

....

....

....

....

....

....

....

....

....

TAKE ACTION: Plan an hour this week to do one or a few of these things that put your mind at peace.

List 5

LIST THE BEST CHOICES YOU
HAVE MADE IN YOUR LIFE SO FAR

....

....

....

....

....

....

....

....

....

....

....

....

....

TAKE ACTION: Take five minutes each morning this week to reflect on your list before you start your day. You have so much to take joy in; trust in your inner wisdom.

List 6

LIST THE THINGS (FROM YOUR PAST AND PRESENT)
THAT FEEL LIKE BLOCKADES IN THE WAY OF HAPPINESS

....

....

....

....

....

....

....

....

....

....

....

....

....

....

....

....

....

....

....

....

....

....

....

....

....

....

....

TAKE ACTION: Look back at List 5 and see if any of your past great decisions can influence how you handle the things that currently stand in the way of your happiness.

List 7

LIST THE GREATEST COMPLIMENTS AND ENCOURAGEMENT YOU HAVE EVER BEEN GIVEN

....

....

....

....

....

....

....

....

....

....

....

TAKE ACTION: Rewrite your favorite compliment on a sheet of paper or print it out in a font you love. Then tape it to a wall or frame it in your home so that you are reminded every day to choose happiness and self-love.

List 8

LIST THE THINGS YOU LIKE TO DO
THAT DON'T INVOLVE TECHNOLOGY

....

....

....

....

....

....

....

....

....

....

....

....

....

TAKE ACTION: It's easy to end up spending a lot of time with technology, but does that time really make you happy? Take a half hour each day this week that you would normally spend on screens to do something else that you enjoy. View it as your happiness practice time!

List 9

LIST ALL THE LITTLE THINGS THAT HAPPENED
TODAY THAT BROUGHT YOU JOY

....

....

....

....

....

....

....

....

....

....

TAKE ACTION: Every day this week write down one thing that brought you bliss on a little slip of paper, then place them in a jar. Keep this jar of joy going all year, and any time you feel down, dip into the jar to remember the little things that bring you happiness!

List 10

LIST THE WAYS THAT YOU FEEL LUCKY

....

....

....

....

....

....

....

....

....

....

....

....

TAKE ACTION: This week hide something special in a secret corner of your neighborhood: place a crystal along a popular path, hide five dollars under a park bench, or leave an encouraging note in a library book for someone to find. Your love will bring them that feeling of luck!

LIST THE THINGS THAT MADE
YOU HAPPY AS A CHILD

....

....

....

....

....

....

....

....

....

....

....

....

....

TAKE ACTION: Is there anything you used to do as a child that you think you might still enjoy? Pick one thing to try again this week, from rereading a few of your favorite childhood stories to building a pillow fort or kicking a soccer ball around with friends in a park.

List 12

LIST THE PEOPLE WHO MAKE
YOU FEEL HAPPY

....

....

....

....

....

....

....

....

....

....

....

....

....

....

TAKE ACTION: Contemplate what it is about these people that makes you feel so uplifted. Set a date to spend time with or chat with one of them this week.

List 13

LIST THE THINGS IN YOUR LIFE
YOU ARE ACTUALLY ABLE TO CONTROL

....

....

....

....

....

....

....

....

....

....

....

....

....

TAKE ACTION: Cross off anything that involves other people. Ultimately the only things you are going to be able to control are your own actions and choices, and you'll feel better if you can spend less time worrying about the things you can't control. If you feel stressed this week, look at this list and allow your mind to focus on what you can control in a healthy manner rather than what is outside of your control.

Acknowledge

List 14

LIST EVERYTHING YOU FEEL
PASSIONATE ABOUT

....

....

....

....

....

....

....

....

....

....

....

....

TAKE ACTION: As Van Gogh said, "I would rather die of passion than of boredom." Everyone has a deep-down something that they feel passionate about or desire. Sometimes your passion conflicts with who you think you are or it feels difficult to attain with your busy schedule. Plan an afternoon this month that you will devote to exploring and investing in your deepest passion without fear or embarrassment!

LIST THE THINGS YOU WANT
TO SAY NO TO

....

....

....

....

....

....

....

....

....

....

....

....

....

....

....

....

....

....

....

....

....

....

....

....

TAKE ACTION: Did you include the words *fear* or *guilt* on your list? So often we spend so much time worrying about whether to say yes or no to a person or an experience that we get lost in guilt and worry. It's ironic since the root of having a hard time saying no is that we are afraid of feeling guilty! This week follow your gut and practice saying no to the things you don't have the time, energy, or desire to do. Skip the guilt phase and enjoy feeling assured of your choices!

List 16

LIST THE EXPERIENCES THAT HAVE MADE
YOU FEEL YOU ARE LIVING LIFE TO THE FULLEST

....

....

....

....

....

....

....

....

....

....

....

....

....

....

....

TAKE ACTION: Can you take the joy and excitement of these events and re-create them on a smaller scale? If you feel like it's doable, go wild and try one of these things in your everyday life this week.

List 17

LIST THE MOVIES, BOOKS, AND TV SHOWS
THAT MAKE YOU FEEL HAPPY

....

....

....

....

....

....

....

....

....

....

....

....

....

....

....

....

....

....

....

....

....

....

....

....

....

....

....

....

TAKE ACTION: Tomorrow morning wake up a half hour earlier than normal and read your favorite book, or watch part of your favorite movie or TV show. It's so much more fun waking up to indulge in what you love than waking up to do tasks!

List 18

LIST THE THINGS ABOUT YOURSELF THAT
YOU *DON'T* NEED TO CHANGE

....

....

....

....

....

....

....

....

....

....

....

....

....

....

....

TAKE ACTION: Set a reminder on your phone or calendar to reread this list on this day one year from now to remember all of the ways that you do love yourself and are proud of who you are!

List 19

LIST THE WAYS THAT YOU THINK SOMEONE
YOU LOVE WOULD DESCRIBE YOU

....

....

....

....

....

....

....

....

....

....

....

....

TAKE ACTION: Now go ask them to list their favorite elements of who you are and compare your list to theirs. Don't be shy; it will make them so happy to tell you why they love you!

LIST THE HAPPIEST PEOPLE YOU KNOW

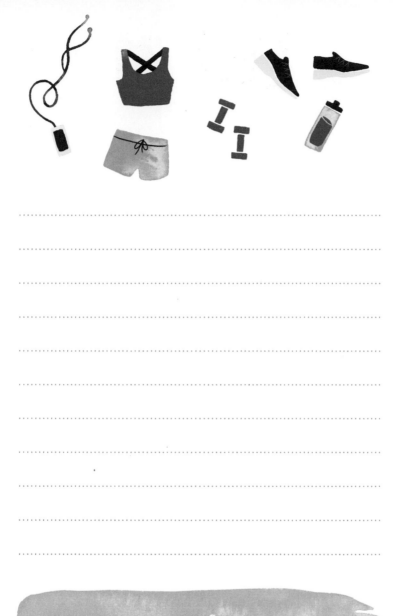

....

....

....

....

....

....

....

....

....

....

....

TAKE ACTION: How do these people express their happiness? This week try emulating the way that someone you admire expresses their positivity and joy. It might feel uncomfortable or weird at first, but practice makes everything easier!

List 21

LIST THE BEST OPPORTUNITIES THAT OTHERS
HAVE GIVEN YOU THROUGHOUT YOUR LIFE

....

....

....

....

....

....

....

....

....

....

....

....

....

....

TAKE ACTION: Gratefulness is such a huge source of happiness. Write a letter this week thanking one person whose kindness has given you an opportunity to grow.

LIST THE THINGS YOU PRIORITIZE BEFORE DOING WHAT REALLY MAKES YOU HAPPY

....

....

....

....

....

....

....

....

....

....

....

....

....

....

....

....

....

....

....

....

....

....

....

....

....

....

....

TAKE ACTION: Make a new list with happiness as the number one priority, followed by your other weekly goals and chores. Post this list on your refrigerator. Look at it every day and set the intention of happiness first, then see how you feel at the end of the week!

List 23

LIST THE SIMPLE WAYS YOU ENJOY BEING KIND TO OTHERS

....

....

....

....

....

....

....

....

....

....

....

....

....

TAKE ACTION: Turn this list into a checklist and see how many ways you can be kind to others this week. Mark off each item that you complete!

List 24

LIST EVERY COLOR YOU CAN THINK OF AND
WHAT MOOD YOU ASSOCIATE WITH EACH COLOR

....

....

....

....

....

....

....

....

....

....

....

TAKE ACTION: Focus on your happiest color this week. Every time you see that color, acknowledge the feeling that it brings you and make it a goal to bring that color into more elements of your favorite space.

List 25

LIST THE WAYS THAT YOU ENJOY INVESTING
IN YOUR MIND, BODY, AND SOUL

....

....

....

....

....

....

....

....

....

....

....

....

....

....

TAKE ACTION: This week practice one of your favorite ways of investing in yourself for at least fifteen minutes every day. If you're able to get outside while practicing your self-investment on a few of those days, even better! Breathe in that fresh air, soak up the vitamin D from the sun, and feel renewed.

List 26

LIST THE TIMES WHEN YOU FELT LIKE YOU
MADE A DIFFERENCE IN SOMEONE ELSE'S LIFE

....

....

....

....

....

....

....

....

....

....

....

....

....

TAKE ACTION: Take fifteen minutes today to search the news and social media for people who you think are making a difference in the world. How do you want to emulate what they have done within your own world?

List 27

LIST YOUR VALUES AND BELIEFS

_____

_____

_____

_____

_____

_____

_____

_____

_____

_____

_____

_____

_____

TAKE ACTION: Spend some time today thinking about how your personal values and beliefs integrate into how you live your life at home, how you interact with your friends, and what motivates you at work. Are there elements of your life that aren't aligned with your personal values?

List 28

LIST THE PROJECTS YOU HAVE
BEEN MEANING TO WORK ON AND FINISH

....

....

....

....

....

....

....

....

....

....

....

....

....

....

....

....

....

....

....

....

....

....

....

....

....

....

....

TAKE ACTION: Cross out at least one project that you can let go of for now, then go treat yourself, because letting go is just as much of an accomplishment as starting or completing a project.

List 29

LIST THE HAPPIEST AND FUNNIEST STORIES
AND NEWS YOU'VE HEARD LATELY

....

....

....

....

....

....

....

....

....

....

TAKE ACTION: Spend time this week with a friend or a group of friends, trading the beautiful and ridiculous stories you have heard lately. It's easy to feel bombarded with negative and heartbreaking news with so much access to information these days. But you have the opportunity to flip the dialogue and fill your time contemplating the positive!

LIST THE COMPLIMENTS YOU
WANT TO GIVE TO OTHERS

List 31

LIST THE SPACES IN YOUR LIFE YOU WOULD LIKE TO
CREATE MORE ORDER AND ORGANIZATION IN

....

....

....

....

....

....

....

....

....

....

....

....

....

....

....

....

....

....

....

....

....

....

....

TAKE ACTION: Focus on purging and reorganizing just one area of your home or office this week: your work desk, your kitchen cupboards, a junk drawer, etc. A clean, organized space is a quick way to get your mind at peace, leaving more room for happiness to enter!

List 32

LIST THE WAYS YOU CAN
"FAKE IT TILL YOU MAKE IT" IN BEING HAPPY

....

....

....

....

....

....

....

....

....

....

....

....

....

....

TAKE ACTION: Happiness and positivity take practice. In practicing self-love I once decided to tell myself out loud everyday that I love myself. And you know what? It worked! Practice saying "I'm happy!" out loud every day this week and see what happens!

List 33

LIST THE PEOPLE YOU WANT TO SPEND MORE
TIME WITH BEFORE THE END OF THE YEAR

TAKE ACTION: It is so much easier to experience happiness with the help of a friend. Plan one way you will spend time with a friend this week. Try to keep planning a friend hang-out time once a week for the rest of the year and think of it as your weekly happiness investment!

List 34

LIST THE FOODS THAT TASTE GREAT AND MAKE
YOU FEEL GOOD ABOUT YOURSELF WHEN YOU EAT THEM

....

....

....

....

....

....

....

....

....

....

....

....

....

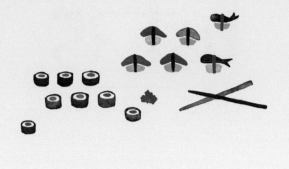

....

....

....

....

....

....

....

....

....

TAKE ACTION: Time for a yummy snack! Go make or buy yourself a snack that makes you feel great emotionally and physically, and tell yourself out loud, "It's treat time!"

List 35

LIST THE ELEMENTS OF YOUR LIFE WHERE
YOU FEEL CHALLENGED IN A POSITIVE WAY

....

....

....

....

....

....

....

....

....

....

....

....

....

....

....

....

....

....

....

....

....

....

....

....

....

....

TAKE ACTION: A life without challenges is pretty dull! Sure, life is comfortable without obstacles but then you don't get the chance to discover new paths to happiness. Pick one challenge, big or small, to focus on overcoming this week.

List 36

LIST THE SCENTS, SPACES, TEXTURES, AND
SOUNDS THAT BRING YOU JOY

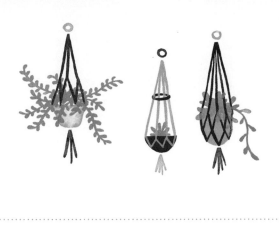

....
....
....
....
....
....
....
....
....
....
....

TAKE ACTION: How many of these things can you combine into one joy-filled experience? Try lighting a candle in the coziest spot in your home, pour yourself a glass of your favorite drink, and indulge in some serious me time with your favorite movie, book, or music.

List 37

LIST TEN WAYS TO GET EXCITED
IN THE NEXT TEN MINUTES

....

....

....

....

....

....

....

....

....

....

....

....

....

....

TAKE ACTION: This is your cheat sheet of ways for you to get positive energy going if you are feeling low and need to get things done! Next time you're feeling low, take a look at this list and take action with one of your favorite positive energy tricks!

List 38

LIST THE THINGS YOU'RE CURIOUS ABOUT

....

....

....

....

....

....

....

....

....

....

....

....

....

....

TAKE ACTION: A discovery starts with first asking questions and allowing yourself to be curious. Pick one of these interests and allow your curiosity to lead you to new discoveries.

LIST THE THINGS THAT YOU
HOPE WILL BRING YOU JOY THIS WEEK

....

....

....

....

....

....

....

....

....

....

....

....

....

....

....

....

....

....

....

....

....

....

....

....

....

....

....

TAKE ACTION: Review this list at the end of the week, and using the blank list pages in the back of this journal, make a second list describing what moments were actually your happiest. What surprised you in exceeding or changing your expectations of happiness?

transform

List 40

LIST THE THINGS THAT FELT IMPORTANT
FIVE OR TEN YEARS AGO BUT ARE UNIMPORTANT NOW

....

....

....

....

....

....

....

....

....

....

....

....

....

....

....

TAKE ACTION: Phew! Doesn't it feel good to recognize all of the things that just don't matter anymore? Visit FutureMe.org and write yourself an email describing what you hope to not worry about in the future and what you are proud of right now. Set a date to receive it around five years in the future!

LIST THE WAYS MONEY *CAN* BUY HAPPINESS

....

....

....

....

....

....

....

....

....

....

TAKE ACTION: Give yourself a small budget this week to buy yourself something that makes you feel awesome, whether it's a new book, a spa day, or paying someone else to do a chore that you dislike. Treat yourself!

List 42

LIST THE WAYS MONEY *CANNOT* BUY HAPPINESS

....

....

....

....

....

....

....

....

....

....

....

....

....

....

TAKE ACTION: Choose one way this week that you will create happiness in your life without buying anything. The sky is the limit!

List 43

LIST HOW WHERE YOU ARE RIGHT NOW FULFILLS
DREAMS AND DESIRES OF YOUR PAST

....

....

....

....

....

....

....

....

....

TAKE ACTION: What are some other dreams from your past that you would still like to fulfill? Choose one way this week to explore one of your childhood dreams and see how it inspires you!

List 44

LIST THE GIFTS YOU WANT TO GIVE TO OTHERS
THROUGH ACTIONS, WORDS, AND WHAT YOU CAN MAKE

List 45

LIST THE THINGS, PEOPLE, AND EXPERIENCES YOU WANT TO SAY YES TO

....

....

....

....

....

....

....

....

....

....

....

....

....

TAKE ACTION: Do you ever hold yourself back from an experience that could bring you happiness? Try saying yes to one thing that is a little outside your comfort zone this week and see how it feels.

LIST ONE ACHIEVEMENT, BIG
OR SMALL, EVERY DAY THIS WEEK

....
....
....
....
....
....
....
....
....
....
....
....
....
....

....

....

....

....

....

....

....

....

....

....

....

TAKE ACTION: Every achievement is valuable! Take pride in your choices, efforts, and achievements, whether they are as simple as getting out of bed or as complex as solving world hunger. Use the blank list pages in the back of this journal to start a second list of how these achievements make you feel about yourself and your life.

List 47

LIST EVERYTHING THAT YOU THINK OF
AS A TREAT FOR YOURSELF

_____

_____

_____

_____

_____

_____

_____

_____

_____

_____

_____

_____

TAKE ACTION: On little slips of paper, write down all of your favorite treats (whether they are actions, snacks, or activities) and place them in a jar. At the end of each week moving forward, pull out a slip and treat yourself, just because!

List 48

LIST THE THINGS YOU THINK YOU'LL WANT
OUT OF LIFE FIVE YEARS FROM NOW

List 49

LIST THE THINGS YOU ARE READY TO RID YOURSELF OF,
THINGS IN YOUR HOME, IN YOUR CLOSET, AND IN YOUR HEART

....

....

....

....

....

....

....

....

....

....

....

....

....

TAKE ACTION: Let's do it! Pick one thing to get rid of in your home, one thing in your closet, or one thing you've been holding onto emotionally this week. Wherever you start, let it be the symbol for a new beginning of feeling freed from the things that drag you down.

List 50

LIST SOME IMAGES THAT MAKE YOU HAPPY

....

....

....

....

....

....

....

....

....

....

....

....

....

....

....

....

....

....

....

....

....

....

....

....

....

TAKE ACTION: Create a collection of photographs, drawings, stickers, paint swatches, and anything that puts a smile on your face. Collect these images in a Pinterest board, a folder on your computer, or a scrapbook or notebook.

List 51

LIST THE WAYS YOU HAVE INVESTED
IN YOUR HAPPINESS THIS YEAR

....

....

....

....

....

....

....

....

....

....

....

....

....

....

TAKE ACTION: Circle the things that you want to continue to do in the year ahead!

Your Last List of the Year!

LIST THE HAPPIEST MOMENTS OF YOUR YEAR

....

....

....

....

....

....

....

....

....

....

TAKE ACTION: You did it! Fifty-two weeks' worth of your truest joy has been discovered, established, harnessed, and cultivated! How many of your happiest moments of this year were things you created on your own? And how many were spontaneous and unexpected? As you look forward into the years ahead, think of this book as your happiness resource. And trust that your life will always hold happiness for you because of two important things: your powerful efforts in the pursuit of happiness and the unpredictable beauty of the world that surrounds you. As hard as life may be at times, there will always be something to spark joy if you seek it. Keep engaging in your own happiness pursuits and embrace the unknown as happiness waits for you around every corner.

Keep it going

Need more room to continue your lists? Or do you have more ideas for other lists you want to make? Add your own lists here to keep the happiness momentum going!

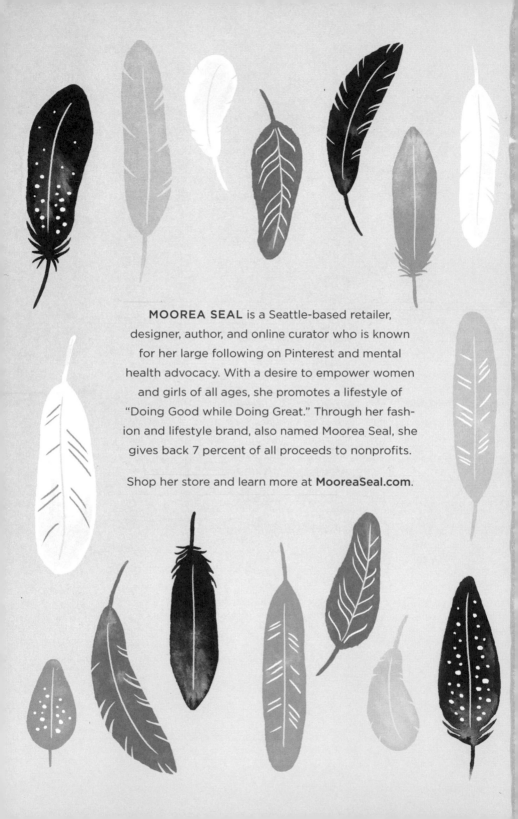

MOOREA SEAL is a Seattle-based retailer, designer, author, and online curator who is known for her large following on Pinterest and mental health advocacy. With a desire to empower women and girls of all ages, she promotes a lifestyle of "Doing Good while Doing Great." Through her fashion and lifestyle brand, also named Moorea Seal, she gives back 7 percent of all proceeds to nonprofits.

Shop her store and learn more at **MooreaSeal.com**.